YOUR KNOWLEDGE HAS VALUE

- We will publish your bachelor's and
  master's thesis, essays and papers

- Your own eBook and book -
  sold worldwide in all relevant shops

- Earn money with each sale

Upload your text at www.GRIN.com
and publish for free

Bibliographic information published by the German National Library:

The German National Library lists this publication in the National Bibliography; detailed bibliographic data are available on the Internet at http://dnb.dnb.de .

This book is copyright material and must not be copied, reproduced, transferred, distributed, leased, licensed or publicly performed or used in any way except as specifically permitted in writing by the publishers, as allowed under the terms and conditions under which it was purchased or as strictly permitted by applicable copyright law. Any unauthorized distribution or use of this text may be a direct infringement of the author s and publisher s rights and those responsible may be liable in law accordingly.

Imprint:

Copyright © 2016 GRIN Verlag, Open Publishing GmbH
Print and binding: Books on Demand GmbH, Norderstedt Germany
ISBN: 9783668329195

This book at GRIN:

http://www.grin.com/en/e-book/342495/cultural-bias-in-the-3rd-edition-of-the-interchange-students-book-2

Elsayed Mahmoud

Cultural bias in the 3rd edition of "The Interchange" (Students' book 2)

GRIN Publishing

GRIN - Your knowledge has value

Since its foundation in 1998, GRIN has specialized in publishing academic texts by students, college teachers and other academics as e-book and printed book. The website www.grin.com is an ideal platform for presenting term papers, final papers, scientific essays, dissertations and specialist books.

Visit us on the internet:

http://www.grin.com/

http://www.facebook.com/grincom

http://www.twitter.com/grin_com

Cultural bias in the Interchange Third Edition (students' book 2)

Table of Contents

1. Background of the Study

1.1 Introduction

The interchange third edition book has been chosen in this study because it's a fully revised edition of new interchange, the world's most successful English series for adult and young adult learners. As per my long experience in teaching this book in the Middle East, I am one of admirers of this book because it is simple, modernized and it also has valuable information to the learners. The author mentioned in the book that English is not limited to a culture, religion or nationality and it's a global or international language. Consequently, It's very important to know whether the aims of the book have been achieved or not. And because the textbook has a strong effect on the learners' behaviors, It is very crucial to be evaluated culturally in order to know whether it is really suitable for our learners or not.

1.2 Statement of the Problem of the Study

As the adapted textbook is considered a linking joint between the English plan and teaching Assessment (Williams1983), While Mariani (1987) mentioned that the textbook stands as a connector between the English materials and the teaching situation, it is worthwhile to carry out an overall evaluation of New interchange third edition and explore whether the previous mentioned English textbook meets the cultural aims and goals stated or not.

Depending on the current controversies that studying a foreign language is considered a part of gaining cultural acknowledgment which it forms, this paper investigates the cultural bias in the interchange textbook 2 through Washington models for the evaluation of bias content in instructional materials and highlights the cultural awareness in it in order to avoid cultural bias in this book and other materials. This paper highlights the uninteresting parts of the instructional materials that are not suitable to the learners' cultural differences. It also presents some recommendations to help the syllabus designers, teachers, institutes to avoid cultural bias in the textbooks.

1.3 Purpose of the Study.

In order to take advantage of the developmental value of the summative evaluation, this study intends to conduct an overall evaluation of the interchange textbook in terms of assessing its main strength and weakness of its relevance and bias to the culture at achieving the following goals:

- Conducting an overall culturally evaluation of New interchange book, third edition, across an American model, ethnic, biased language, gender, omission, perspective and other types, .
- Proposing alternatives to the cultural bias in the book to contain all cultures, western and eastern presented equally in the textbook.

- Eliciting the implications of the strengths and weaknesses of the textbook and proposing recommendations to its writer to adjust it.
- Providing a set of recommendations to the Syllabus designers to avoid cultural bias in the textbooks.

1.4 Significance of the Study.

This study is considerably significant because it provides the textbook authors, teachers, and students and institutes with valuable information culturally about Interchange third edition which is currently considered the most successful series in the Middle East. It also provides the institutes' administrators with an overall evaluation with strong and weak culture's relevance and bias of the EFL materials they are currently using or developing and pedagogical implications for the design of ESL textbook will be suggested. This study used an American model for evaluation of bias content in instructional materials which is set for teachers, students, institutes administrators, and the textbook authors with a significant qualitative method.

1.5 Questions of the Study.

This study tries to find out responses to the following questions:

- Are different and relevant cultures in regards of the books' content presented on an equal footing between western and eastern culture?
- Does the course book contain stereotypes of images or unsatisfied pictures of gender, language, social class, Perspective, omission, or nationality to the origin culture of the book or to the eastern culture?

1.6 Limitations of the Study.

This study was limited for the following reasons

First, interchange third edition student's book (2) has been chosen out of four series of Interchange third edition which are intro, Book1, book2, book3. These are considered one of the most important and valuable series in this century because the sales of these series have achieved unbelievable numbers, as you cannot easily find any of these series in the book shops in the Middle East.

Second, Only the Washington Model for the evaluation of bias content in the instructional materials has been chosen and applied to the above mentioned book. Among many models, this Model has been chosen for its accuracy, comprehension and adaptability to this study.

2. Literature Review

Four decades ago, the learner centered instructional form has been come up and gradually most textbooks have been adapted in parallel to it (Brown 1995). Thus, selecting a course book is very crucial because first, a huge amount of money will be spent for years, second, its influence on students, teachers and learning experience is very important, and third, once you choose one of the textbooks, you cannot retreat (Cunningsworth 1995).

The literature suggests that teacher might depend on their intuition when making course planning decisions more frequently than on the data collected which reflects the learners' needs (Barkhuizen 1998); however the course book has to be evaluated and its evaluation has to reflect the needs of the learners and the aims, methods, and values of the teaching program.

Evaluation may be defined as "a systematic process of determining the extent to which instructional objectives are achieved by pupils" (Gronlund 1981, p.5). There are two important aspects of this definition. First, note that evaluation implies a systematic process, which omits casual, uncontrolled observation of pupils. Second, evaluation assumes that instructional objectives have been previously identified. Without previously determined objectives, it is difficult to judge clearly the nature and extent of pupil learning. While Hutchinson and waters (1987) focus on the evaluation's features by mentioning it is basically a straightforward and analytical. Straightforward means it should be clear including the judgment and the reasons combined with the treatment suggestions. Analytical means matching the process.

White (1988) stated the types of evaluation are distributed into two categories. The first category is formative, While the second category is summative. The formative evaluation is internal and run during the course. On the contrary, the summative evaluation is external and run after the course is finished.

Cunningsworth (1995) stated that there are four steps in evaluation, First, Analysis-which is collecting data-, second, Interpretation of the data collected- issues and priorities are examined-, third, evaluation which is value judgments of learner and teacher expectations, methodology, needs and so on, Fourth, selection which means matching the demands and needs of the learning situation with the result of the previous steps, However McDonough and shaw (2003) suggested that ELT materials evaluation could be implemented in two integrated steps which are the external and internal steps. The external steps include the print, the visual material, vocabulary list, the presentation, and cultural bias and relevance of the material, while the internal steps include the presentation of the skills, materials' grading and sequencing and integration of the materials. Nunan (1988) suggested some points in the evaluation which answers many questions for us. First, the areas which should be evaluated in the textbook are initial planning process & needs analysis, selection & grading of content, program goals & objectives, learning activities, implementation & methodology, resources & materials, teacher performance, students' achievement, assessment and evaluation. Second, the evaluation makers could be at the macro level such as governmental bodies and funding agencies, or at the Local level such as the institutes' decision makers and teachers, or the Learner-centered context such as teachers & learners, and others such as external expert, curriculum employees, and teacher's partners. Third, the convenient time of the evaluation could be at any time from the planning stage onward. Fourth, the evaluation could be conducted by various instruments and strategies such as standardized tests, questionnaires, interview, schedules, and observation schedules for classroom interactions.

Peacock (1997) presented a course book evaluation checklist which is distributed into eight sections. One of the most important sections is the Cultural differences. He set some important points about cultural differences in the course book. First, the availability of cultural bias depends on the learners' points of view. Second, whether a non-western culture depicted as well as the American cultures in the textbook. Third, whether cultural tone eventually convenient in your culture or not.

Skierso (1991) pointed out that the cultural presentation is one of the items has to be considered in evaluating the textbook by asking about whether the textbook differentiates between the American and British English in consideration to the lexis, grammar and structures and if any, how big it is.

6

Cunningsworth (1995) determined four guidelines for evaluating a textbook. First, Course books ought to reflect the learners' needs. They ought to meet the targets and content of the course. Second, Course books ought to be reflective to the uses of the learners to the language. Third, Course books should consider the needs of the students. Fourth, Course books should play a supportive role for learning. They must engage the learner to the target language, But Litz (2005) formed a teacher textbook evaluation which classified into seven categories; First, Practical consideration such as the price of the textbook or the accessibility of the textbook. Second, the layout and design such as vocabulary list and the sequences of the content should be appropriate. Third, the textbook activities such as the individual, pair and group work, should be balanced. Fourth, the skills such as the deductive and inductive skills should be harmonized and balanced. Fifth, the language type such as grammar, vocabulary items functions convenient to the target language. Sixth, the subject and content should be relevant to the target language's cultures in order not to be rejected by them. Seventh, conclusion; the appropriateness and convenience of textbook for the language-learning aims of my institution should urge me as a language learner to study it again.

Williams (1983) pointed out that the target language and the mother tongue are different culturally and causing problems in learning a second language. And one of the factors that textbook writers have to consider is the relevance of its culture while specifically Sheldon (1988) stated some criteria in evaluating ELT textbooks and materials. One of the most essential criteria is the cultural bias. And there are some important questions in this specific criterion. Are varied religions and societies depicted in the book? Are the learners' aspects to the content, educational methods presented equally? Are offensive or stereotypes of gender, race, social class and nationality available in the textbook?

As the cultural bias in education is available through Academic modules and some texts (Baker, 2005), many researchers consent that academic content should be made by different members of cultures (Gay, 2000; Rogoff, 2003).

Sonia (2008) pointed out that the definition of culture is not easy and causing problems as it has specific meaning to various groups in a diverse situation, eg. Culture converted from referring to what the high class people do in their leisure time into everyday's situations. As culture is different from a group of people to another, American's culture is different to European's culture or African Americans'. And the relationship between culture and education is complicated, as there are differences between the learners culturally.

Although the definition of culture is not easy, it might be defined by Banks as "an interrelated system of ideas, values, symbols, products, behaviors and so forth all function together interdependently" Banks (2006).

Karen (2003) expressed that human beings have diverse cultural and lingual families. This diversity is useful to Americans, not only in the physical environment, but also in the notions, fancy and intangible statements, however the culture bias of the whites has been available and if it continues, it will have a negative effect on the Americans, not to be limited to, separatism.

A review by Potvin et al. (2009) stated that learners have got a system-specific gender bias in rating their science teachers. Males and females learners rated their males and females teachers who teach chemistry, physics and biology to them. Male students undervalued the female teachers while the female students overvalued their female teachers except for the physics teachers and as known there's a lack of females in this field. This clear gender bias might influence female learners negatively and support the permanent unavailability of females in science, technology, engineering, and mathematics fields.

Ndura (2004) expressed that ESL students' learning and experiences are greatly affected by the educational content. Consequently, textbooks and other educational stuffs should not only reflect one culture to the immigrant students but also reflect diverse cultures, so that they can engage their perspectives and avoid cultural bias in the educational process by some suggested strategies.

3- Methodology

3.1 Models to be applied

Washington models for the evaluation of bias content in instructional material have been used in this significant study. They are used because they are considered as comprehensive guidelines for evaluating educational stuffs with a close concern to a bias of race, gender, culture, religion and others.

3.2 Materials to be evaluated.

The New interchange third edition students' book (2) has been examined in regards of receptive and productive skills. This book is designed for adult and young adult learners. It contains 16 units. Each part contains modern content of English materials. It has multi-strands syllabus with focus on the communicative approach.

The authors of these textbooks are Jack C. Richards, Jonathan Hull and Susan Proctor. They have revised the new interchange book and have issued the new interchange third edition series as a result of the fast growing of English learners and the success of these series between the learners.

3-3 Criteria for identifying bias:

As the many cultural perspectives are important in our curriculum, it has to be presented the different aptitudes, stances and models in the educational stuffs, and not to immortalize them by giving more or less intention to specific groups or life models.

The contemporary stereotypes are affiliated with the following:

- Race
- Gender
- Socioeconomic
- Family make-up
- Native Language
- Lifestyle

- Ethnicity
- Religion
- Disabling condition
-
- Occupation

- Cultural bias could be explained in the above mentioned terminologies through the examples beneath:

Stereotypes (Ethnic – Sexual – Other types)
Ethnic

A specific group of people are successful and rich while other groups or a country are presented as a group of riots, working in low positions as waiters, having no jobs, and wearing poor clothes.

A currency of specific people is available with humiliating other currencies. Some specific group or race is successful without dividing the success between many groups.

Chinese Americans are depicted as living only in Chinatowns or doing laundry and other Asians, not to be limited to, Filipinos, presented as waiters, loan mowers and Japanese are only presented as people wear only one type of clothes shared in the Second World War. Specific groups are presented only as migrants, sleepy or low class, while others are stable, active and high class.

Sexual

Boys are presented as active and able to manage themselves without needs of others, while girls are presented as observer. Women are presented as stupid, tamed, concerned with minor things or nonsense, while men are presented as brave, wise, and or struggling to be successful or winners.

Other types

Nuclear family groups are only depicted with a successful father, house wife, and two or four kids. People of specific classes or nationalities eat specific kind of food, wearing a type of clothes. People with special needs presented with sticks or wheels car. Specific groups of people are presented to be better in some skills than other groups. White people presented to be more athletic than blacks. Couples are presented as young not a family.

Biased language

Present vocabularies which belong to some specific people or the majority without checking their acceptance for the minority or other groups culturally or religiously. Unpopular group of people are presented by only the first names while popular people are presented by the whole name or title. Present the majority or specific names of western without presenting other people's names and or eastern names. Present some subjects to the adult or the young adults which are not accepted by other cultures. Humankind is presented by males and some sentences don't include females. Various phonetics not presented. Various terminologies are misused.

Omission

Only European-American life models are presented while others life models are not presented. Unpopular and women's participations in some fields, not to be limited to, History, Science, and so on, are not presented in some parts of the textbook. Unpopular group members are excluded from the context. Present western places and omit eastern land marks.

Perspective

Unpopular groups or women are not familiar with the technology while popular groups or mend are so familiar with them. Certain people are identified or presented just in terms of their rapport to other people such as MR. Jones' wife Sara. Elderly people presented as not able to perform as adults or youths. White citizens are presented to be so proud of being white and modernized while African Americans have dark-colored environment and primitive. Some specific group of people enjoys welfare or luxury while other groups are not stable or have no luxurious life or services. Women behave like men.

4. Findings and Data Analysis

Ethnic

It is seen in the book that three people considered the three successful people in the world. The first one is Michael Jordan. The second one is Madonna Louise. The third one is William Henry. According to the above mentioned model, there are all American and the book doesn't present some western successful people.

It is also seen that the American currency is the only currency in the book while it's appear in the conversation the American man doesn't know the

European currency and doesn't mentioning Eastern some currencies or notes.

In the book Honk Kong people are only depicted as waiters. According to the model, the book should present them both in high and low positions.

Sexual

It's found in the book that the girl is crying and needs a help of the policeman while the questions are asking about positive features, while the man is able to manage his work himself in the picture stands next to it. Culture bias is seen in the former and latter pictures because according to the American model, girls are not brave and need others while men are able to manage work themselves.

It's found also in a picture in the book that a man is happy and self confident while a woman is so frightened of the animal. According to the American model, it's a kind of bias to present boys with only positive features and girls with only negative features.

Other types

It's found in the book that Nuclear family, which is parents, and one to 4 kids, only depicted in the book while single family, which is only a young couple, is not depicted. And there is no extended family which has a wider family, parents, grandfathers, grandmothers, grandsons and relatives and according to the American Model, it's culturally biased.

Biased language

Vocabularies: Although the writer paid attention to the vocabularies which are culturally biased in the second edition, not to be limited to, Champaign, frog's legs and omit them in the third edition, It's found in the book some words which are culturally biased, not to be limited to, Pork, girlfriend, boyfriend, date someone. According to the American model culture bias has occurred because they are not accepted culturally to the eastern, especially the Muslims.

Names: It's found in the book that all the names in the book are Western, Not to be limited to, Albert, Daniel, Pete, Tanya and no eastern and Arabic names. According to the American Model, the book doesn't have to present only group of people or the majority and leave the minority.

Subjects: It's found in the book that some topics are accepted only in the western country, not to be limited to, Love and fall in love. According to the American model, it's a kind of culture bias because these subjects are not accepted culturally.

Phonetics: Only the American pronunciation and accent are depicted in the book. According to the American model, the book has a culture bias because it doesn't present the British accent and people from Eastern countries speak in the right way with their accents.

Omission

It's found in the book that all ladies wear the Western clothes and without scarf. The book presented only western life without presenting the eastern life to give a balanced life of all groups. According to the American model, it's a kind of culture bias.

It's also found in the book that the famous land mark is western and no eastern famous land marks available. According to the American Model, It's a kind of culture bias because it omits the eastern culture when highlights the famous landmark.

Perspective

In the listening part of the book, the woman has a slight problem with the computer and unfamiliar with using the computer, so she calls the call center and the man has solved it with just pressing any key or moving the mouse to disappear the screen saver, while in the same part, there is a conversation section, the woman wants to borrow the man's mobile because she has no mobile at all and doesn't know how to use it to call her boss. The man gave her the mobile and explained how to use it. According to the American Model, it's a kind of culture bias because of the above mentioned information.

It's found in the book that elderly people are not working and enjoying the life only without positive activities, while the youth and adults have positive activities. According to the Washington models, it's a kind of culture bias because it presents the elderly as they are not able to perform as the youth or adults.

5. Discussion

As the ascending needs to the textbooks for few decades, they must be evaluated carefully and be reflexive to the learners' needs. The evaluation could be either summative or formative. From this summative analysis, Learners have to know the meaning and the examples of cultural bias in the textbooks.

It is also learnt from this paper analysis and findings that new interchange book (2) has many cultural biases either for the country of its origin and the eastern countries. The students, teachers, institution's administrators and the syllabus designers have to know the influence of cultural bias on the learners and try to avoid it. All groups or nationalities have to be treated equally in the textbook.

6. Summary and Recommendations

6.1 Summary

The results indicated that According to the Washington Models, the authors tried in the new edition to avoid some vocabularies which are culturally biased, However, According to the American Models; there are a lot of criteria prove that the book contains many examples of culture bias until now.

The finding through the Washington Models also revealed the culture bias to the authors, institutes' administrators, teachers, students to know the book's strength which is obvious through the materials and the multi strands syllabus which have been used, and the weakness which are obvious through the Washington models and its criteria.

6.2 Recommendations

In light of the findings of the study, the following recommendations and pedagogical implications were implied to the syllabus designers to avoid culture bias in the textbooks as follow:

1- All ethnic groups should be portrayed equally in this textbook and other international textbooks.
2- Successful stories, heroes from the Eastern culture as well as the western culture should be presented in this textbook and other international textbooks.

3-The textbook should contain Eastern famous names, subjects, life styles and landmarks as well as westerns'

4- All types of families, not to be limited to, single, extended, nuclear families, should be presented in this text book and other international textbooks.

5- Both genders "males and females" presented with positive and negative features or merits equally.

6- Cultural data and information have to be collected about the target language by questionnaires, interviews or other media methods.

7- Syllabus designers should use modern technology such as the computer software to help to identify culture bias for the target language.

8- Identify the stereotyped images or offensive illustrations in the textbook in order not to be rejected by different cultures.

9- Identify the book's perspectives to know whether it presents only one side perspective or include Western and Eastern perspectives.

10- Look at copyright dates of the books whether they are after or before 1970s because the books which are issued before 1970s were not distinguishing between the genders or paying attention to the cultures in their materials.

As Adrian Holiday (1992) warned from the troubles that cultural bias can make because of irrelevance of the cultures between the foreign employees and the host institution requirements and will cause tissue rejection, it's seen that the textbook loaded with cultural bias will have the same effect on the local learners. Hence the syllabus designers, authors, teachers, institutes decision makers have to pay much attention to the culture in the textbooks.

7. References

Baker, P. (2005). The impact of cultural biases on African American students' schooling. *Education and Urban Society*, vol. 37 (3), pp. 243-256.

Banks, K. (2006). A comprehensive framework for evaluating hypotheses about cultural bias in educational testing. *Applied Measurement in Education*, vol. 19 (2), p. 2.

Barkhuizen, G. (1998). Discovering learners' perceptions of ESL Classroom teaching/learning activities in a South African context. *TESOL Quarterly*, vol. 32 (1), pp. 85-108.

Brown, J.D. (1995). *The elements of language curriculum*. Boston: MA: Heinle.

Cross, K. (2003). Analysis of Life Curriculum for White Cultural Bias. *Religious Education*, vol. 98 (2), pp. 239-259.

Cunningsworth. A. (1995). *Choosing your course book*. Macmillan Education Bookstore. pp. 8-18.

Douglas, M. (1982). *In the Active Voice*. London: Routledge & Kegan Paul.

Gay, G. (2000). *Culturally responsive teaching*. New York: Teachers College Press.

Gronlund, N. (1981). *Measurement and Evaluation in Education*. New York: Macmillan. p. 5.

Holliday, A. (1992). Tissue Rejection and Informal Orders in ELT Projects: Collecting the write information. *Applied Linguistics,* vol. 13(4), p.405

Hutchinson, T. and Waters, A. (1987) *English for specific purposes.* Cambridge: Cambridge University press.

Litz, D. (2005). Teacher Textbook Evaluation Form. *Asian EFL Journal,* pp. 43-45.

Mariani, C.F. (1987). Course Maintenance; the Problem and Solutions. *Education Technology,* vol. (12), pp. 28-32.

McDonough, J. & Shaw, C. (2003). *Materials and Methods in ELT.* Edingurg: Blackwell publishing.

Ndura, E. (2004). ESL and Cultural Bias: An Analysis of Elementary through High School Textbooks in the Western United States of America language. *Culture and Curriculum,* vol. 17 (2), pp. 143-153.

Neito, S. (2008). Culture and Education. Yearbook of the National Society for the study of Education, vol. 107 (1), pp.127-142.

Nunan, D. (1988). *The Learner centered curriculum.* New York: Cambridge University.

Potvin,G., Hazari, Z., Tai, R. & Sadlar,P. (2009). Unraveling Bias from Student Evaluations of Their High School Science Teachers. *Science Education,* vol. 93 (5), pp. 827-845.

Rogoff, B. (2003). The *cultural nature of cognitive development.* New York: Oxford University Press.

Sheldon, L. (1988). Evaluation ELT textbooks and materials. ELT Journal, vol.42 (4), pp. 237-245.

Skierso, A. (1991). *Textbook selection and evaluation.* In M. Celce-Murcia (Ed.), Teaching English as a second or foreign language. Boston, MA: Heinle & Heinle Publishers.

Washington office of the state superintendent instruction. (1996). *Washington models for the Evaluation of bias content in instructional materials*, pp. 4-9.

White, R. (1988). *The ELT Curriculum Design.* Oxford: Blackwell Publishing.

Williams, D. (1983). Developing criteria for textbook evaluation. *ELT Journal*, vol. 37 (3), pp. 251-255.

YOUR KNOWLEDGE HAS VALUE

- We will publish your bachelor's and
  master's thesis, essays and papers

- Your own eBook and book -
  sold worldwide in all relevant shops

- Earn money with each sale

Upload your text at www.GRIN.com
and publish for free